FAST Lane
OPEN-WHEEL RACING

INDY CARS

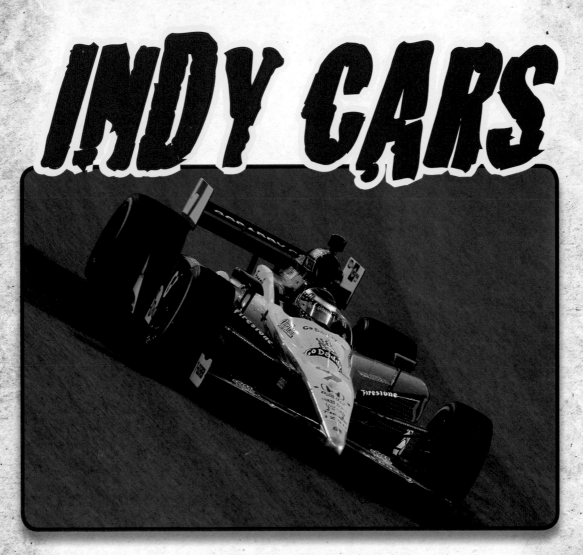

By Tyrone Georgiou

Gareth Stevens
Publishing

Please visit our website, www.garethstevens.com. For a free color catalog of all our high-quality books, call toll free 1-800-542-2595 or fax 1-877-542-2596.

Library of Congress Cataloging-in-Publication Data

Georgiou, Tyrone.
 Indy cars / Tyrone Georgiou.
   p. cm. — (Fast lane. Open-wheel racing)
 Includes index.
 ISBN 978-1-4339-5756-7 (pbk.)
 ISBN 978-1-4339-5757-4 (6-pack)
 ISBN 978-1-4339-5754-3 (library binding)
 1. Indy cars—Juvenile literature. 2. Automobile racing—Juvenile literature. I. Title.
 TL236.G462 2011
 629.228—dc22

                            2010052709

First Edition

Published in 2012 by
Gareth Stevens Publishing
111 East 14th Street, Suite 349
New York, NY 10003

Designer: Daniel Hosek
Editor: Greg Roza

Photo credits: Cover, p. 1 Nick Latham/Getty Images; pp. 4–5, 17 Jonathan Ferrey/Getty Images; pp. 5 (Guthrie), 9 (old race car) Racing One/ISC Archives/Getty Images; pp. 6–7, 8–9 (main image), 14 Robert Laberge/Getty Images; p. 7 (engine) Shutterstock.com; pp. 10–11 David Taylor/Getty Images; p. 13 (both images) Chris Graythen/Getty Images; p. 15 Ron Hoskins/Getty Images; p. 19 Rick Dole/ Getty Images.

Printed in the United States of America

CPSIA compliance information: Batch #CS11GS: For further information contact Gareth Stevens, New York, New York at 1-800-542-2595.

CONTENTS

Words in the glossary appear in **bold** type the first time they are used in the text.

LET'S GO INDYCAR RACING

IndyCar is the top open-wheel racing series in the United States. Races take place at tracks across the country as well as in Brazil, Canada, and Japan. Unlike other open-wheel series, it takes place on oval tracks, super speedways, and road courses. IndyCar drivers come from many different countries. The biggest race of the year is the Indy 500, which has been held on Memorial Day weekend since 1911.

Fast Fact Both men and women **compete** in IndyCar. The first woman to compete was Janet Guthrie in 1977. In 2011, there were five women regularly competing.

Janet Guthrie

Danica Patrick, shown here during the 2010 Indy 500, was the first woman to win an IndyCar race.

WHAT'S AN INDY CAR?

An Indy Car is an open-wheel car with an uncovered space, or cockpit, where the driver sits. It's built to a special set of rules. All teams race the same type of car. A company named Dallara makes the frames. In 2012, Chevrolet and Lotus joined Honda in making engines for the cars. Each team tries to get an advantage over other teams by making small changes to the **aerodynamics** and **mechanical** parts. This makes for close finishes!

Fast Fact

The Honda **V-8 engine** was used in all Indy Cars produced before 2012. It ran on 100 percent ethanol, which is a fuel made from corn.

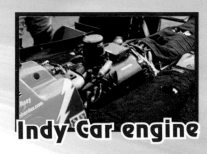

Indy-Car engine

Scott Dixon of New Zealand fights to stay in the lead at the 2010 Indy 500.

IndyCar racing goes back to 1906. Back then, it was called Champ Car. The first national championship was held in 1916. In those days, drivers competed in many different kinds of cars on tracks made of dirt, bricks, and **asphalt**. Some tracks were even made of wood planks, or boards!

The modern Indy Car took shape in the 1970s and 1980s. The engine is behind the driver. Wings and other aerodynamic parts help increase the cars' speed and handling on asphalt racetracks.

Fast Fact

As auto racing became popular in the early 1900s, tracks made of wood planks were created. These tracks were very unsafe. By the 1930s, they were all gone.

Driver Joie Chitwood raced in the Indy 500 seven times in the 1940s. He later performed in the Joie Chitwood Thrill Show.

BUILDING A BETTER INDY CAR

Through the years, several notable Indy Cars ruled the tracks. In the 1920s and 1930s, race car builder Henry Miller made V-8 engines for many teams. Fred Offenhauser—who once worked for Miller—built an engine that helped many teams win the Indy 500.

In the 1960s, the Lotus company's new lightweight cars changed the way race cars were made. The Lola company combined cutting-edge parts and advanced aerodynamics to create cars that **dominated** IndyCar in the late 1980s and 1990s.

NASCAR legend Robby Gordon also raced Indy Cars. Here he leads the 1996 Las Vegas 500K.

Fast Fact Between 1912 and 1937, a mechanic could ride with the driver in each Indy Car!

CHAMP CAR CHAMPS

A.J. Foyt—known as "Super Tex"—raced everything from midget cars, to stock cars, to sports cars. He won the Champ Car series seven times and holds the most Indy 500 wins with four.

Mario Andretti won four IndyCar championships. He's second in all-time IndyCar wins with 52. He has 111 career wins across many types of auto racing.

Helio Castroneves won the Indy 500 three times between 2001 and 2009. He's famous for climbing the safety fences after winning.

Helio Castroneves climbs the safety fence after winning the Indy Japan 300.

Helio Castroneves

13

THE INDY 500

The Indy 500 is raced on a 2.5-mile (4 km) oval track built in 1909. The track is called the Indianapolis Motor Speedway and is in Indianapolis, Indiana. The surface was originally paved with bricks. Today, the track is called the Brickyard even though only a small strip of bricks remains. The rest of the track is now asphalt.

original bricks

"Indy 500" is short for "Indianapolis 500-Mile Race." IndyCar **qualifying** speeds reach 225 miles (362 km) per hour and faster.

Ray Harroun won the first Indy 500 in 1911. His average speed was 74.6 miles (120 km) per hour. Dario Franchitti, the 2010 winner, had an average speed of 161.623 miles (260.107 km) per hour!

The Indy 500 is often called "The Greatest Spectacle in Racing." A spectacle is an impressive display or event.

Franchitti's car

Harroun's car

THREE DAYS AT THE INDY 500

The Indy 500 happens at the end of May. In the middle of May, drivers start practicing.

- Qualifying Day—This happens the weekend before the race. Each driver gets three laps around the track. The fastest driver wins the **pole position**.

- Bump Day—This happens the day after Qualifying Day. There are only 33 spots. If you're not fast enough, you're out.

- Race Day—Race day is 200 laps of all-out racing. The winner drinks milk in the winner's circle!

Fast Fact

On speedways, teams use smaller wings to get the most speed. On road courses, larger wings create greater **traction** to get around corners more quickly.

Drinking a bottle of milk has been an Indy 500 tradition since 1936. That year, winner Louis Meyer actually had a bottle of buttermilk after winning the race.

CHANGES IN INDYCAR

Beginning in 2012, IndyCar introduced new car **specifications**. While Dallara is still building the body frames, other companies can now create their own aerodynamic features. Instead of V-8 engines built by Honda, Indy Cars now use special V-6 engines built by several companies. Chevrolet and Lotus are two companies building the new engines, which has brought these historic racing names back to the series. Some changes were made to make Indy Cars better for the **environment**.

The "pits" is the place where cars refuel and get fixed during a race.

Fast Fact In 1967 and 1968, the STP team ran cars powered by turbine engines. Turbines are jet engines. However, the cars were not dependable. They never finished a race.

19

TODAY'S TOP DRIVERS

Dario Franchitti began his racing career in the British Formula 3 series. He holds two IndyCar championships and two Indy 500 victories.

Brazilian Tony Kanaan has one championship and 14 wins since 1998, but he's still waiting for his first Indy 500 win.

In 2008, Scott Dixon was the first driver from New Zealand to win the Indy 500. He also has two IndyCar championships and 24 wins. Danica Patrick was the first woman to win an IndyCar race.

INDYCAR NUMBERS

Most IndyCar wins	A.J. Foyt, 67
Most IndyCar championships	A.J. Foyt, 7
Most Indy 500 wins	A.J. Foyt (1961, 1964, 1967, 1977) Al Unser (1970, 1971, 1978, 1987) Rick Mears (1979, 1984, 1988, 1991)
Fastest lap ever at Indianapolis Motor Speedway	Arie Luyendyk, 1996, 239.260 miles (385.052 km) per hour

GLOSSARY

aerodynamics: the properties of a car that allow air to slide over it easily so it can move faster

asphalt: a natural matter used to make roads

compete: to try to win a contest with others

dominate: to be better than all others

environment: the natural world in which we live

mechanical: having to do with machines

pole position: the best starting place for a race, decided by the fastest qualifying time

qualifying: having to do with time trials that decide which drivers will be in the main race and what position they will start in

specification: a detailed rule about how to make or do something

traction: the stickiness between two surfaces, such as a tire and the track

V-8 engine: a motor where two banks of four cylinders each are arranged in a V shape

FOR MORE INFORMATION

Books

David, Jack. *Indy Cars*. Minneapolis, MN: Bellwether Media, 2008.

McCollum, Sean. *Indy Cars*. Mankato, MN: Capstone Press, 2010.

Pimm, Nancy Roe. *Indy 500: The Inside Track*. Plain City, OH: Darby Creek Publishing, 2004.

Websites

Indianapolis Motor Speedway

www.indianapolismotorspeedway.com

Read about one of the greatest speedways in the United States and find out about upcoming events.

Izod IndyCar Series

www.indycar.com

Find out the latest IndyCar news.

INDEX